QUADRIGAs
MICROCOMPUTER WORLD

Rolf Lohberg • Theo Lutz

MEET THE MICRO

a beginners guide to personal computers

Illustrations: Gerhard Utecht

QUADRIGA PUBLISHERS

MEET THE MICRO

First published in Great Britain by Quadriga Limited 1984
Warwick House, 334 Kilburn High Road, London NW6 2QN, England

Also in the same series published by Quadriga Limited

Now ready

Make the most of your Pocket Calculator
BASIC-Programming made simple

September 1984

Teletext for Everyone
Computers in the Home
Microcomputer Dictionary

British Library Cataloguing in Publication Data

Lohberg, Rolf
Meet the micro.—(Quadriga's microcomputer world)
1. Microcomputers—Juvenile literature
I. Title II. Lutz, Theo III. Utecht, Gerhard IV. Heim Computer.*English*
001.64.'04 QA76.52

ISBN 0-900608-18-8

Foreword

During the past few years the computer has come within reach of almost everyone. It would be hard to find more than a handful of people throughout Europe, the United States and Japan who have never encountered a computer, even if only in the shape of a pocket calculator. Not that this development is anything new in the world of modern technology: just think how the telephone, television, washing machine and dishwasher have become a part of so many households.

But there are other reasons for the recent computer boom. Before computers could sell in such large numbers, manufacturers had to find ways of making them not just smaller but cheaper. The result is that you can go into a shop today and buy a portable computer which can do every bit as much as the giant mainframes of a decade ago. Yet your new computer will have cost only a fraction of the price of its predecessor.

Added to this is the fact that certain computers have been designed for use by the average businessman with little or no specialist training in data processing. These are the personal computers or microcomputers — and these are what this series is all about. In this book we tell you what sort of personal computers exist, how they work and what you can make them do for you. We also tell you what to look out for when buying a computer — either for yourself or as a gift.

contents

What is a computer?

The microcomputer or personal computer

Computers come in a great many shapes and sizes. At the top of the range are the powerful 'main-frames' used in industry. They are followed by 'minicomputers', and then by 'microcomputers', so-called because they contain a microprocessor. This book deals only with microcomputers — the 'home' or 'personal computers' designed for your own use in home, office or classroom. As you can see from the pictures on this page, not all personal computers — or micros — look the same.

The floppy disk

As its name implies, this is a disk made of very thin plastic with a coated magnetic surface. It is enclosed within a plastic envelope from which it is never removed. The floppy disk enables you to record and play back programs and data far more quickly than on a cassette. You can also find a specific program far more easily than is possible on a cassette. To use a floppy disk, you slide it through a slot in the front of a disk drive, a device which acts rather like a record-player.

The print

The handbook

Even the greatest computer expert needs to refer to a handbook or manual once in a while. No two computers are identical in all respects, so it is vital that the handbook accompanying you PC is accurate and easy to follow. Remember: study the handbook carefully before attempting to use the computer!

The keyboard

Every personal computer has a keyboard. It is used for typing data, programs and commands into the computer. The keyboard is very important because it is the means by which you communicate with the computer. Though similar in many ways to

The memory and the microprocessor

The nerve centre of the computer is the Central Processing Unit, or CPU. It consists of a microprocessor and a number of support units which enable it to function. In order to work the computer needs a series of instructions such as 'print', 'add', or 'read a number'. We call a series of instructions like this a program.
The memory (or 'work memory') can take in data, store them and release them again when needed. The memory also contains the program for the processor, which has been fed in by typing it on the keyboard. When something is typed in on the keyboard, it appears on the screen for control purposes, but it is not really inside the computer until it has been stored by the memory.

You will find that different books refer to microcomputers by various names: home computers, personal computers (PCs) and so on. In this book the term microcomputer is used for preference.

The screen

All personal computers need a screen. Information which has been fed into the computer is shown on this screen, and anything the computer works out appears here too. this 'output' may consist of individual numbers, or tables, or words, or even moving pictures. So the screen is a piece of equipment for outputting data.
Larger and consequently more expensive home computers have their own screen, or Visual Display Unit (VDU.) The picture may be colour, or black and white.
Sometimes the screen is built into the computer.
Cheaper home computers are usually designed to be connected to an ordinary television set. In this case you can either watch television OR use the computer, but not both at the same time.
Very small home computers look rather like pocket calculators. Instead of a screen they have a single-line display for 20 or more characters.

A new vocabulary

A great many new words and technical terms have come into everyday use as a direct result of the computer boom. Without a knowledge of this new vocabulary you cannot learn to use a computer.

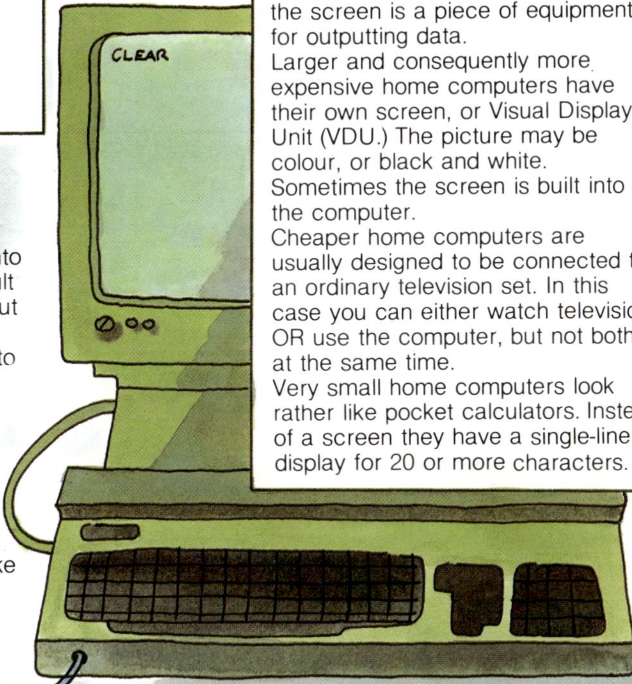

he printer is an utomatic typewriter onnected to the omputer. It provides a ecord in words and/or umbers of everything e computer produces. ome printers can even rint pictures.

The information produced can be filed for later use and, unlike the picture on your computer screen, it does not disappear when the power is switched off.

an ordinary typewriter, he computer keyboard usually has a number of extra keys. Whatever you 'input' or type onto he keyboard appears on the screen. The keyboard is the most common method of nputting data to the computer.

Cassettes

Ordinary audio cassettes, like the ones used to play and record music, are widely used for storing computer data. First, you record ('save') your programs onto tape, then you play them back ('load' them) into the computer. Cassettes are a cheap way of storing programs, but they are slow to use. Each time you want to retrieve some new data you have to rewind the tape to the beginning and start all over again.

The computer program

Step by step

A program is a set of instructions telling the computer what to do and when to do it. For example, a washing machine program determines when water is to be pumped in and to what temperature it should be heated. A computer program stipulates in what way the different parts of the computer are to work together to solve a particular problem. It tells the computer when to expect which data, how they are to be processed, and when to produce a print-out.
A program consists of individual steps. These are called instructions, commands or orders. These instructions can be words, but there are also special symbols like + which means add together, or * which means multiply. These symbols and key words help to make programming easier than it may at first appear.

A very simple example

Our aim is to write a short program using the number of kilometres driven by a vehicle, and the litres of petrol used, to work out the fuel consumption per 100 kilometres:

```
1   READ KILOMETRE, LITRE
2   CALCULATE CONSUMPTION = LITRE/KILOMETRE * 100
3   PRINT CONSUMPTION
```

The instructions are given running numbers. If you know that / means divide and * means multiply, you can understand the program and work it out for yourself.

Programming languages

In order to enter programs into your computer, you need to use a language it can understand. There are in existence a number of 'high-level programming languages' designed to be easily understood by the user. The computer, however, can only understand what are known as 'machine languages'. So the user's programs in a high-level language have to be translated by the computer into its own machine code. With home computers this job is done by the microprocessor. It translates the program and then carries it out step by step.

In this book we will use only one programming language. It is common to many personal computers and is called BASIC which stands for Beginners All-purpose Symbolic Instruction Code. It has the advantage of being very easy to understand. Some pocket calculators use it too.

Instructions

Using instructions in BASIC our example looks like this:

```
10  INPUT KILOMETRE, LITRE
20  LET CONSUMPTION =
    LITRE/KILOMETRE*100
30  PRINT CONSUMPTION
40  STOP
```

The symbols =, / and * belong to the language of BASIC, as do the words INPUT, LET, PRINT and STOP. They are known as keywords. BASIC has approximately 50 keywords. The programming manual tells you which words

ıriables

ery piece of information to be processed must have its 'n individual 'name'. These names are known as ıriables'.

variable used to store a number is called a 'numeric riable' or a 'simple variable'. They are represented by a ter, but you can also add a figure if you prefer. So ›SIC names for numbers could be K or L or M6. If you pe in your program

LET K6 = 100

en as of this instruction the variable has a value of 100. riables that hold words rather than numbers are called ring variables' and are written after a dollar sign. So in e expression

LET Z$ = "SMITH"

e name SMITH is stored in the Z string variable. The ote marks " " indicate the beginning and end of the ing.

Our example in BASIC

We are now going to write our petrol consumption program in a more refined form of BASIC. To do this we need to observe the rules regarding names, and allocate a number to each line. These are usually at intervals of 10 to allow for later insertions if necessary.

```
10   INPUT K,L
20   LET C = L/K*100
30   PRINT C
40   STOP
50   END
```

At STOP the program pauses, and by inputting 'END' we tell the computer we no longer need a memory. Later we will learn how to make a program 'user-defined'.

Question: What is the rate of consumption if K = 359 km and L = 32.51? The microcomputer will rapidly work out the answer to 9 places after the decimal point.

ıta and instructions in the memory

e memory's job is to record data — not y information, but also lists of tructions. Every character is allotted a emory cell in the personal computer. e microprocessor has a list which tells it which cell the first character of every name can be found, and how many cells are occupied by the whole name. The same applies to the instructions except that here the number plays the role of the name. Every cell in the memory has a kind of house number. This is called an 'address'.

an be used on your articular computer. It lso explains exactly what an instruction neans, and teaches you o write it correctly.

f you do not follow the ules exactly (for example, if you omit ommas or other unctuation marks) the nicro cannot carry out s instructions. It will hen stop and print a nessage on your screen elling you what is vrong.

Each line of commands egins with a number nown as a 'line umber'. These control he order of the list of nstructions.

The memory

Computers have memories that can store many thousands of characters. We therefore refer to their capacity in units of thousands of characters (or bytes) at one time. The unit used for this is the kilobyte, which is often shortened to kbyte,or even just K. A capacity of 48,000 bytes, or 48K, is a good size for a personal computer.

Most microcomputers have two kinds of memory. One is called ROM. The characters in this memory are there for good, and cannot be changed. The other memory is called RAM. You can feed characters into this memory yourself.

What is a ROM?

ROM is short for Read Only Memory. As its name implies, it is a memory which can only be read from, and not written into. It can be compared to a book or a record. It is loaded with information by the manufacturer of the micro and contains everything that the computer needs to operate. For example, the program which translates BASIC instructions into machine language is usually in the ROM. 16K ROM is usual for a microcomputer.

What is a RAM?

RAM is an electronic memory which you can write into and read from — as on a tape, for example. RAM is short for Random Access Memory, and means that you can write into or read from every cell at random. All data input by the computer, for example from the keyboard, go to the RAM. So the RAM is a sort of notebook. An important point to remember is that the RAM is 'volatile'. This means that unless data are 'saved' in one way or another, they are lost when the power is switched off.

Using the keyboard

The keyboard

The keyboard allows you to input data, programs and commands into the computer. Sometimes it is an integral part of the screen, but it may be attached separately.

The input is fed in character by character — as with a typewriter. If you press 'K', the keyboard sets off a sequence of electrical impulses which represents 'K' for the computer. The 'K' is stored in a register and appears simultaneously on the screen. Having typed a series of characters which the computer is to store, you then press an input key (usually called 'ENTER'). when you press this key, anything you have typed is then stored in the computer (probably in the RAM).

All microcomputers have keys for the letters A-Z, the figures 0-9, and punctuation marks. They also have a number of extra keys for special functions, like the ENTER key.

Dual-purpose keys

Some keys have a double function. For example on the lower half of one key there is a '4' and on the top half the sign '$'. As on a typewriter, if you depress the key marked 'SHIFT' at the same time as the key marked '4' and '$', only the '$'is printed. The 'SHIFT' key can be locked in position, in which case only the symbols on the top halves of the keys will be printed. The same happens when you require capital rather than lower case letters. many microcomputers can only display capital letters on the screen, but some can print lower case letters too.

Spaces

The space between two words, the 'blank', is usually achieved by pressing a spacebar (as on a typewriter keyboard).

The cursor

A smaller screen can display up to 2,000 characters — about the same as a page of double-spaced typing on A4 paper. The cursor shows which of the 2,000 possible positions is being selected at any given moment? It is a small flashing square, or other signal which moves on one space each time you type a character.

Moving the cursor around the screen

On many keyboards there is a series of special keys which position the cursor on the screen without needing to write any characters. These are marked with arrows to indicate the direction in which they will move the cursor. Keys marked 'NEW LINE', 'RETURN' or 'ENTER' also move the cursor.

Input errors on the screen

If you have typed in an error, you must move the cursor back and print over the mistake. Be careful: on a typewriter the space-bar does not affect what you have already typed. On the screen, however, it cancels an existing character and replaces it by a blank.

Function control keys

Microcomputers have a number of special keys known as function control keys. These can be used together or separately to give access to all its features. They vary from one machine to another.

The joystick

Some micros have a port to which control levers called joysticks can be fixed. These move the cursor at will, and are needed for certain computer games.

Printouts

If your micro has a printer, you can direct it to produce its output in the form of a printed sheet.

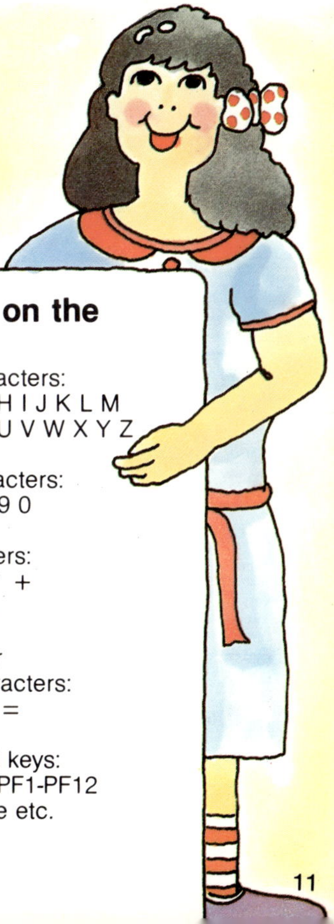

Characters on the keyboard

Alphabetic characters:
A B C D E F G H I J K L M
N O P Q R S T U V W X Y Z

Numerical characters:
1 2 3 4 5 6 7 8 9 0

Special characters:
! $ & / ( ) = ? * +
' £ - __ : . ; , #

Alphanumeric or alphameric characters:
A to Z and 1 to =

Function control keys:
ENTER, SHIFT, PF1-PF12
Arrows, Advance etc.

The microcomputer as desk calculator

On some keyboards (usually on the right hand side) you will find 16 additional keys in 4 rows of 4. These carry the figures 0-9, a decimal point, and symbols for addition, subtraction, division and multiplication. These keys enable the computer to be used as a desk calculator. This can be useful if the micro is on your desk anyway, and you want the facility to carry out simple calculations.

ENTER

When you press the ENTER key (which can also be called RETURN), anything which has been typed in and appeared on the screen passes into the computer RAM.

Our first real program

User-defined and interactive

It is now time to put our program for working out fuel consumption per 100 kilometres into a more sophisticated form, so that it will do the following:

1 Let us know what it wants to hear from us.
2 Comment on what it is doing.
3 Keep on picking up and adding data pairs (number of kilometres and litres until all the pairs have been processed.

The steps that make up this program are explained on this page. The program is written in BASIC, but remember that your computer may use a different dialect. Consult your manual! The prompts that the program produces are 'user-defined'. Compared to the original version, it is now also 'interactive'.

Keywords

The following keywords appear in our program:

=	A name is given a value.
PRINT	Something is printed or appears on the screen.
INPUT	Input is requested from the keyboard.
+	Two numbers are added together.
IF	A condition is checked.
GOTO	Branch.
LET	Calculation; the result is given a name.
*	Two numbers are multiplied together.
STOP	Program flow is finished.
END	End of the program.

1 — Preparation

he names L (Litre) and K Kilometre) are continuously o be added to. First the lata names must be given he value 0. (L = 0 and (= 0). The data which were tored up until now under hese names are cancelled. f these are characters, then paces must be left in their lace.

```
:0
=0
                              1
NT "ENTER
OMETRES AND LITRES"
UT K1, L1
                              2
= K + K1
L + L1
                              3
NT "MORE DATA? (Y/N)"
UT F$
F$ = "YES" GOTO 20            4
T C = L/K*100
NT "CONSUMPTION
R 100 KM"; C                  5
OP
D
                              6
```

2 — Data input

As the data input is to be user-defined, the computer tells the user by means of a PRINT instruction which data it expects from him. The text following the word PRINT is a character string, and it is printed and displayed on the screen exactly as it appears between inverted commas.
K1 and L1 pick up the data pairs via the INPUT instruction — acting like a kind of intermediate memory.

3 — Processing

The data values requested via INPUT are added to the variables K and L. This is the purpose of the two 'add' instructions K = K + K1 and L = L + L1.

4 — Checking and branching

At line 40 the user is asked to tell the computer whether more data pairs are to be expected. If he types in 'YES' or (Y), then the whole run is repeated from the beginning. At line 45 a 'YES' is expected, or otherwise something that counts as a 'NO' or (N). The answer is stored under F$.

At 47 the 'IF' command checks whether the answer is 'YES'. If so, the program flow is put back to command 20 by means of the GOTO.
If the answer is not 'YES', the program carries on, the 'IF' has no effect and command 50 follows next. This possibility of deciding between two different courses of action is what we call branching.

5 — Evaluation

At 50 the microcomputer knows that no further data pairs are on their way. You now print a 'LET' (not necessary in some BASIC dialects). The computer can work out the fuel consumption per 100 kilometres. At the 'PRINT' command, it prints out the answer on the screen.

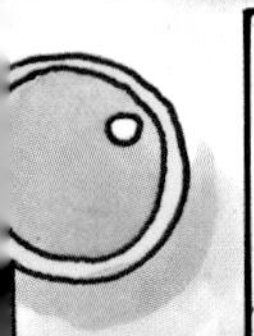

6 — End of program

When no further calculations are required, the 'STOP' command is given.

The sequence of instructions

There aren't many rules to remember about allocating line numbers. The important thing is that they must indicate the sequence in such a way that there is no room for confusion. Gaps are left between the numbers so that you can slip in further instructions later on if you wish.

A flow chart

If you were to trace the flow of control through a simple program, it could look something like this on the screen of a microcomputer. On the left is what is typed in, and to the right is what the computer says:

```
RUN
   ENTER KILOMETRES AND LITRES
   ?
325
   ?
30.2
   MORE DATA? (Y/N)
   ?
YES
   ENTER KILOMETRES AND LITRES
   ?
409
   ?
38
   MORE DATA? (Y/N)
   ?
   NO
   CONSUMPTION PER 100 KM
   9.291553134  BREAK AT 60
```

Entering a program into the computer

Entering the commands

It's usual to start by writing down your program on a piece of paper, so that you are quite clear about what instructions to give. You then type in your commands so that they enter the memory. As you already know, a command consists first of a line number which may have between one and four digits. This is followed by a space, and only then do you type in the specific command. In BASIC, this always starts with a keyword. Every computer has a number of features designed to make typing easier.

These are known as 'control keys', and include the cursor and the keys which enable it to move freely.

Typing

Make sure the screen is clear before typing a new program. Your handbook will tell you how to achieve this.
Start by typing in the first line number, follow it with a space and then key in the command. when you are satisfied that there are no errors, press the ENTER key. This causes the computer to take control of the command and store it. Further commands are entered in the same way, although you do not need to clear the screen each time. What is important is to ensure that the line numbers get bigger with each line of command.

Line numbers

In our example on the previous page we wrote the line numbers in such a way that we could immediately see which command they referred to. This is done for the sake of convenience.

It is equally important to remember to type in the line numbers in tens, rather than in single units. In other words, count 10, 20, 30 rather than 1, 2, 3. That way you can enter further information later on. You will find out how to do this under the heading 'Inserting commands'.

Many computers give you line numbers automatically, which is very useful. More about this under the heading 'Auto'.

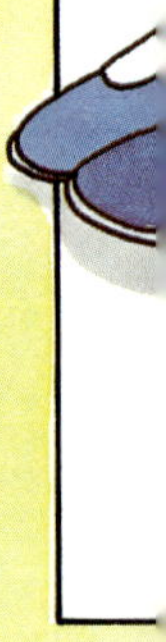

Print

It is usually advisable to check your program. To do this type in

LIST (ENTER)

This command causes the program in the memory to appear on the screen. If the program is longer than the screen, your computer will have a facility for moving the text up the screen. If your micro has a printer, you can have a printout at the same time. Many computers have a special function key enabling it to print out what you see on the screen. It is usually labelled PRINT SCREEN, PRTSC, COPY or similar.

AUTO

This command produces line numbers. Start by typing

AUTO (ENTER)

and the first number will appear on the screen as 10. If you follow this with a command, the next number will appear as 20.
The numbers ascend in tens, for reasons you already know.

Inserting commands

It sometimes happens that you suddenly realize you have left something out of a program. In this case, the missing instructions must be inserted — often by pressing the 'INSERT' key. This is followed by the line number, a space and, finally, the command itself. Many computers will accept a new command with its line number, in which case you do not need to use the 'INSERT' key. But on most machines a new command overwrites the old one, so that you can edit what you have written. Simply type out the correct command, and its line number, onto the screen, and press 'ENTER'.

Deleting commands

In order to remove something from a program, most micros require you to type in 'DELETE', followed by a line number, and to press the 'ENTER' key. Less complicated computers will accept the line number on its own, without the word 'DELETE'. That can be risky, although a lost command can easily be typed in again.

Renumber

Not all micros possess this facility. If you enter this command and your computer understands it, you can completely alter the sequence of commands, starting from 10 and ascending in tens. You now have nine positions free between each two commands, in which you may if you wish insert new commands. Press the 'LIST' key and your commands are now arranged as you like.

This facility of renumbering program commands automatically is very convenient when you are constantly adding new data to your program.

Running the program

In order to test a program, press

RUN (ENTER)

The program will start with the command at the lowest line number and will continue until the STOP command, or until it meets a mistake. The screen will show you where the program has stopped. Most errors stem from faulty programming, a few from incorrect data and only very, very rarely because the machine is malfunctioning.

What is a command?

Commands or instructions are words typed on the keyboard which tell the computer what to do. Commands are used to feed data into the computer, and to process and retrieve data from it. INPUT, LET, PRINT, IF and GOTO are typical commands, as are RUN, and LIST.

The special function control keys on the keyboard also act as commands, and make for more efficient use of the computer.

Why have a cursor?

The cursor helps you find your way around the screen. It is operated by four keys, one for each direction. If you keep a cursor key depressed, the cursor continues to move in that direction until you release the key. The cursor can be used in conjunction with other keys. For instance, you may be able to combine the CURSOR and INSERT keys so that everything on the screen begins to move to the right. You now have a clear space on your screen for new inserts.
Or you might try positioning the cursor on the screen and pressing the DELETE key. Anything to the right of the cursor will start to disappear from the screen. Mastering the cursor is well worthwhile — it is a very valuable friend on the micro's screen.

More memory for your micro

How data and programs are stored

ROM (Read Only Memory) is a kind of storage system from which it is only possible to read (or fetch) data and programs. No new information can be entered into the ROM. Commands in BASIC are stored up to operate the microprocessor. The other kind of storage is RAM (Random Access Memory). It can be both read from and written into, which means you can type your own data and programs into it. The trouble is that each time you write a new program to RAM, it overwrites (erases) whatever was there before. So you need some means of storing programs, and this is where the cassette and floppy disk come in. Using tapes or disks you can record your programs, store them permanently when not in use and play them back with ease whenever you need them.

Programs held in RAM

All instructions start with a line number. A correctly written program begins with the lowest number and ends with the command END. Follow this sequence correctly and your program will be entered into the RAM. Now key RUN and the computer will play your program back. If you are typing in several programs, follow the RUN command with the line number with which the program you want begins. When saving a program on disk or cassette, remember to give it a name. If your program is called MASTER, key SAVE "MASTER". (SAVE is a command, like LIST or RUN.) When you want to retrieve that program from the RAM, key LOAD "MASTER".

Inside the memory

When you enter a line number or a program name, your microcomputer automatically displays the contents of the RAM on screen. This display is normally in BASIC.

Some computers display the contents of the RAM or ROM without translating it into BASIC.

RAM and ROM chips

Chips are tiny wafers of silicon containing minute transistors. A chip no more than a quarter of a centimetre square contains over 100,000 transistors, or room for 8,000 characters. In a 64K RAM or ROM, 8 chips are interconnected inside a plastic or aluminium housing. The whole thing measures only $2.5 \times 2.5 \times 0.5$ centimetres. Each chip has room for around 50 connections.

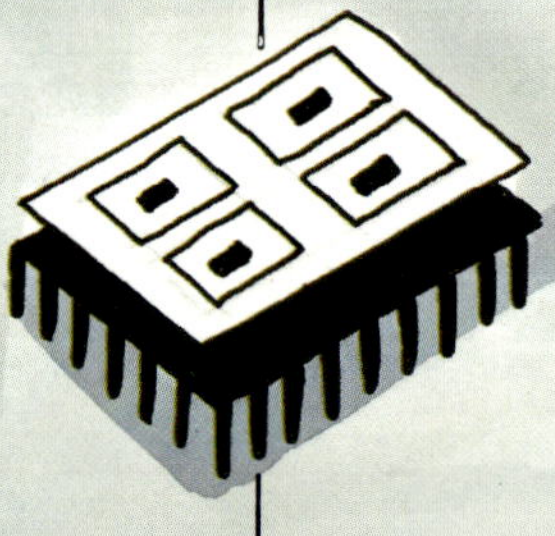

Data in store

BASIC has the facility to allow you to write data into a program. Data statements may be either numbers or letters and are usually written into a program using the DATA instruction. They are retrieved from memory through the READ command. When storing data on disk or cassette it is important to remember to give them a name to make identification easier.

Cassette storage

It is possible to store data on an ordinary music cassette. Some micros have a built-in cassette recorder, but in most cases it must be purchased and attached separately. Your computer manual will tell you which types are suitable for your machine. Ordinary cassettes can store up to 64M characters — i.e., one thousand times the capacity of a 64K computer.

Storing programs on tape

You can record a program as you would a piece of music. When you have typed in your program, insert a blank tape into the cassette recorder, key SAVE, followed by the name of the program and ENTER. The program will be transferred from the RAM onto tape as soon as the 'record' button is pushed. You should keep a notebook telling you the names of programs stored, together with the tape counter numbers.

When you want to replay the program, insert the cassette into the recorder, key LOAD, together with the name of the program, and press the 'play' button. On some computers a message (such as 'OK') appears on the screen, telling you whether the program has been successfully saved on tape. You can listen to the tape of your program if you like — it sounds a bit like some electronic music.

What is a data bank?

For every account a savings bank keeps a record consisting of the customer's name, account number, rate of interest and amount saved. One could write this as:

BANK: NUMBER, CUSTOMER, INTEREST, BALANCE

Such a sequence is called a data line, and several together form a file.

Using a cassette

Data are always written onto a cassette via a program. Items of data are entered individually and can only be read in the order in which they are entered. The code ensures that the program always retrieves the correct item of data.

Thus a data statement in BASIC might look like this:

```
225 DATA BESTBANK, C, N$, I, B
```

To retrieve the data, key:

```
325 READ BESTBANK, C. N$, I, B
```

BESTBANK is the name of the file. It is followed by the data list.

Disk storage

There are considerable advantages in using a disk drive to store data and programs. The floppy disks used are made of plastic with a magnetic coating. A disk is inserted through a slot in the front of the drive, which then rotates it at high speed. The disk's surface is divided into concentric tracks, over which a magnetic read/write head moves back and forth. When you ask the computer to load a particular program, the head moves to the correct track and reads in the program. Disks have a capacity of up to one million characters and mini-floppies, with a 13 cm diameter, can store around 160K. They are very widely used.

Disk sectors

Before you can use a disk it needs to be divided into sectors, or 'formatted'. The data you wish to store are allocated to a particular sector and coded so that they link up with the directory. When an item is selected from the directory, the magnetic head moves immediately to the correct sector. This takes only seconds compared to the minutes needed to find the same information on tape. It also has the advantage that programs can be retrieved in any order, without playing through an entire tape to find a particular item.

Programs on disk

Disks are particularly useful for the safe storage of programs. When you want to transfer a program to disk, key SAVE followed by the name of the program, press ENTER and the rest is done automatically. Similarly, typing LOAD, followed by the name of the program will return the program to RAM so that you can work from it.

The micro shows what it knows

The screen and the printer

The purpose of both screen and printer is to allow you to read data output by your computer. The information remains on screen for only a short while, but can easily be called up again. If it is printed on paper, of course, it provides a more permanent record. Your computer will have a key marked PRINT, but whether this operates a printer, or the screen, or both, depends on that particular micro's capabilities.
To print a message on the screen, type in a line number, then key PRINT followed by your message which must be in inverted commas.

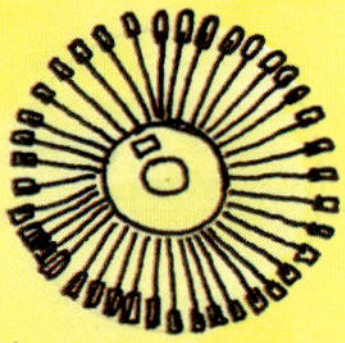

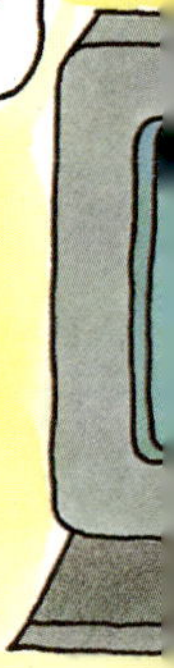

The daisy wheel printer

This printer operates with a plastic wheel with one character or symbol at the end of each spoke. A hammer strikes the appropriate character against a ribbon to produce the printed symbol needed. The printer produces good quality at high speed.

The dot matrix printer

This is a printer that forms letters with a series of dots. The simplest dot matrix printer consists of a line of needles that press ink from a ribbon onto the paper as the head moves across it. It is fast, and comparatively cheap.

The thermal printer

Some dot matrix printers use special heat-sensitive paper. A heating element moves across the paper, and where a hot spot is created a blue dot appears on the page.

The ink-jet printer

Minute droplets of ink are combined, rather like the electron beams in a TV set, to form letter shapes on a particular spot. Ink-jet printers are costly, but they produce good definition on many different surfaces.

Printout paper

The typewriter takes individual sheets of paper which are fed in one at a time. Computer printout paper on the other hand comes either in a continuous roll or in a stack. It has holes punched down both sides to feed it into the printer, and sheets are perforated at intervals so that they can be torn off individually.

Print quality

The quality of the print depends on the paper, the age of the ribbon (where used) and on which kind of printer is employed.

How the screen works

Like a television screen, the screen of a microcomputer may consist of anything between 50,000 and 500,000 picture dots, called 'pixels'. Individual dots can be switched on and off at will. Since they are electronically controlled, this all happens very fast. With a colour screen, you can also choose which areas of dots you want in which colour. The dots can be used to form letters, words, figures and even pictures. If you look closely at the screen you will see that all the words or pictures on it are in fact made up of tiny dots.

How much room on your screen?

Most microcomputer screens are capable of displaying about the same number of characters as would fit on one typewritten page of A4 paper. In other words, some 2,000 characters plus the space between, in 40 rows of 50 letters. We arrive at this figure by dividing the 5 × 7 dot matrix into the number of pixels.

You can print pictures too

Dot-matrix printers can produce complicated characters and even graphics. Each symbol is built up sequentially from the dots. The finer the dots, the sharper the image. Dot matrix printers can build up new typefaces and quite acceptable pictures. Colour dot-matrix printers are also available, but they tend to be expensive and awkward to handle.

The Monitor

The microcomputer's screen is known as a 'monitor' or 'cathode ray tube' (CRT). As we have seen, the images that appear on it are made up of thousands of pixels. The smaller these pixels are, the sharper your picture will be. Ordinary television screens use fairly large pixels, so their pictures are fuzzier than those of a micro monitor.

Picture resolution, or sharpness, is measured in numbers. For example, a picture with a resolution of 180 × 120 means that the screen is composed of 180 horizontal rows of pixels and 120 vertical columns. Some monitors will only show black-and-white pictures, but the best screens can handle up to sixteen colours.

Using your television screen

Some micros can be connected up to a domestic television set. For this you need a special adapter designed to fit into the computer at one end and into the aerial socket of your television receiver at the other.

While you are using the computer, you cannot watch programmes on television.

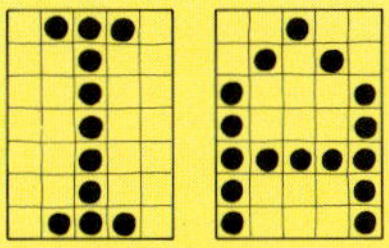

Dots and symbols

Using dots to make numbers, letters and pictures is not a new idea. Just look at a newspaper photograph through a magnifying glass. To produce characters on a screen, your computer uses a matrix. This will generally consist of seven rows of five dots each, and with it you can generate almost all the characters and graphic symbols your computer will need.

Using the figure 1 for 'ON' and 0 for 'OFF', all the characters displayed on the micro can be represented by a succession of 1s and 0s. This is called 'binary' notation. From reading the series of 1s and 0s that represent the character the computer's processor determines which pixels on the screen to switch on and which to leave off. If you move far enough away from the screen you can no longer see the matrix.

Sounds and pictures

Dots, tones and signals

We are now ready to start looking more deeply into the computer and exploring some of the micro's more unusual possibilities. For this, you need a little patience and perseverance.
The symbols which appear on the micro's screen and printouts are made up of dots. Almost all micros are so organized that you can use the dots in whatever way you wish. You can even draw and 'paint' with the micro if it has a computer graphics facility.
To learn more about this you need to study your handbook carefully.

The same applies to sound. It is easy to get the micro to squeak, but less simple to make it produce music, let alone speech.

When you realise that some computers also have the facility to steer your electric train set you will begin to understand what a lot of fun you could have with it.

Co-ordinates

Let us assume that our micro screen has 200 lines of 640 dots each. The lowest row is called the X axis. Along it are 640 dots, from 0 to 639. The left-hand vertical column is called the Y axis. Reading from bottom to top there are 200 dots — from 0 (the first dot of the X axis) to 199. X and Y cross at dot (0,0) — so that the first number in the brackets represents X, and the second Y. Dot (135,419) lies above X-dot 135 and to the right of Y-dot 419. This means you can describe every dot on the screen with two numbers.

From screen to printer

Most micros are so built that you first draw your graphics on screen, and then enter a command ordering it to produce as many printouts as you require.

Computer graphics

These are complex but exciting aspects of computing and call for great care in choosing your micro. You can get low resolution graphics which will draw simple lines and blocks or high resolution graphics which you need for computer games.
Computer graphics are used a lot on television and as a form of art.

Back to graphics

To produce graphics your micro needs the command 'PLOT'. Try the following:

Line number PLOT (X,Y)

In many computers, this will engage the dot with the (X,Y) coordinates. PLOT INVERSE (X,Y) removes the dot. For example: the program

```
10 FOR N = 0 TO 639
20 PLOT (0,N)
30 NEXT N
```

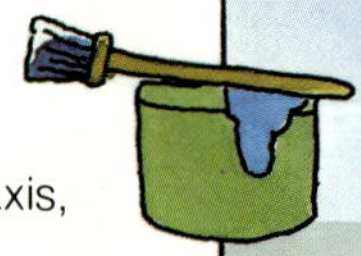

brings in all the dots on the X axis, one after another. The BASIC command FOR enables the commands between 10 and 30 to be used two hundred times.

If your computer understands this program, you're laughing. If not, consult your handbook.

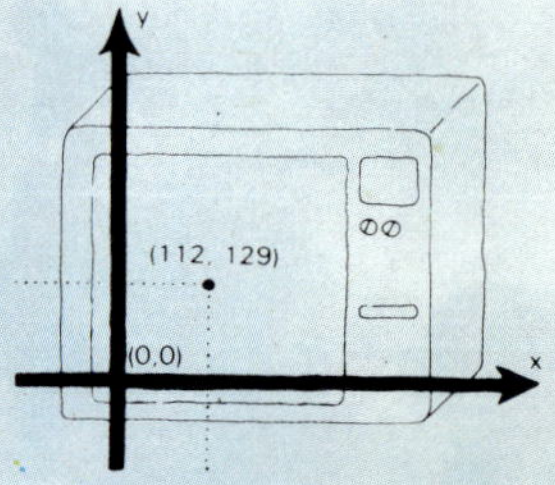

What is a signal?

A red traffic light warns motorists to stop and wait until a new signal appears. The light turns red because an electric current has been switched on. As long as the current is switched on, the signal remains visible.

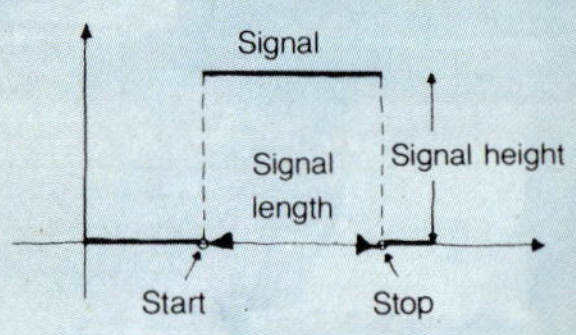

hat is a
ne?

one or note is a
ration of the air.
e strong or weak
nplitudes'
oduced are what
u know as loud or
't notes. At high
quency (with the
vibrating quickly)
u hear a high note
e drawing above
nt). At low
quency you hear a
v note.
any micros
derstand
quency and
nplitude and can
ect the
udspeaker to emit
variety of tones.

Sounds from the computer

Nowadays, a great many low-priced pocket calculators and wristwatches can 'beep' every hour, or be set to wake you with an alarm call. Similarly, many micros possess a small loudspeaker, through which you can hear bleeps. More sophisticated computers have a synthesizer. They can be programmed to produce various sounds — and even to mimic human speech. Many computers also have programs (extended versions of BASIC) which produce pieces of music. In computer language we refer to BEEP, SOUND and MUSIC depending on the type of noise.

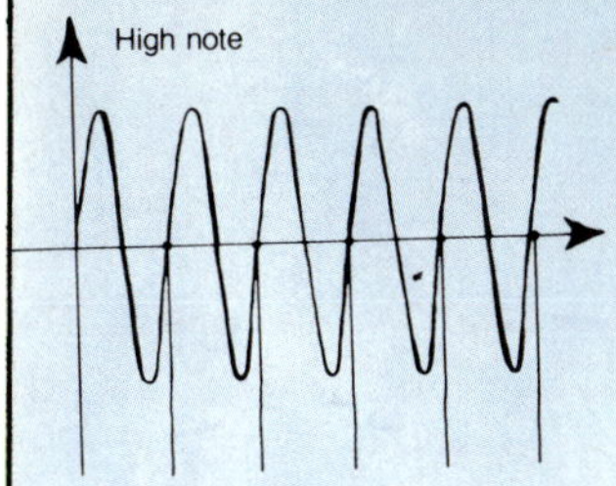

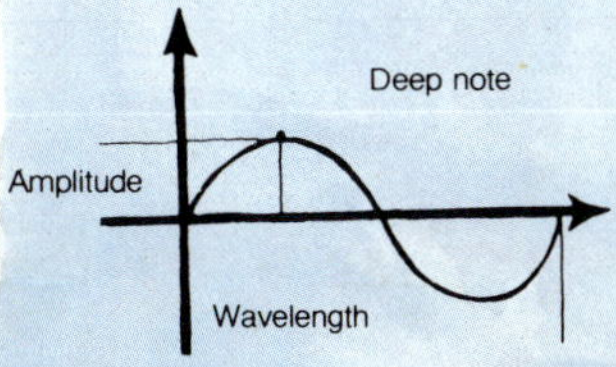

Sound

Only a small number of micros can 'speak'. In any case, to use this facility requires very careful study of the manual. First you have to input various symbols — representing the syllables of speech — into the synthesizer. It in turn balances the frequencies and amplitudes which enable the loudspeaker to produce audible words. However, they tend to sound more like a computer than a human voice. This is bound to improve in future.

Music

Some programs understand symbols based on musical notation. In that case you can feed pieces of music into the computer. The program translates these notes into sounds for the synthesizer. It in turn emits these sounds through the loudspeaker. Not many micros have this facility. Choose your computer with care if you want to compose computer music. But remember that composing is both expensive and time-consuming.

BEEP

Most BASIC dialects understand the word BEEP, though some use another word in its place and a few do not have the facility at all. If you input

425 BEEP 5

the micro will emit five short bleeps on the same note when it reaches line 425. You can use this to draw your attention to a particular part of the program — if you wish to insert something new, for example. Or it can warn you the program is at an end.

omputer signals

the computer is a piece of electronic uipment, it must be able to handle signals. any micros can cope with electrical signals of certain frequency, process them, and produce them as other signals. All that matters that the signal exists: everything else — equency, strength, etc can be electronically gulated. A computer that can handle signals s a junction box for receiving and emitting gnals. It can understand commands from tside — mostly not in BASIC — enabling it to k signals together. All the rest is done through ograms written by the user. Your handbook ll tell you how. Bear in mind that using mputer signals is a job for experts.

Computerised toys

A computer that can receive, adapt and emit signals is the perfect playmate. Many toys and games make use of electronic signals — take the electric train set, for example. A signal is sent, informing the computer that the train has passed a certain spot and that the points are set to 'right' or 'up'. Back comes the signal from the computer, changing the point to 'left' or 'down'.
If you intend using your micro as a signals processor, you must first make sure it is properly equipped. Circuit board components are available which can receive, emit, join together or boost signals. However, they are complicated to insert, and not suitable for beginners.

Bits and other pieces

Measuring information

Most modern motor cars have a dashboard indicator telling you what position the handbrake is in. For example: Light on might mean handbrake on; Light off might mean handbrake off. For 'Light on' you could also say 1 — and for'Light off', 0. Or 'yes' and 'no'.

There is no middle position. Similarly, the microcomputer understands only two positions — On and Off, represented by the digits 1 and 0. Each of these binary digits is called a bit. Using our car example we can see that if we have two bits we have four possibilities 00, 01, 10 and 11. These might be connected to the two headlights the battery and an oil level probe. 00 would then mean: all OK; 01 might be an oil level warning light; 10 could signal a nearly flat battery and 11 might mean the headlamp bulbs were not working. Traffic lights are capable of eight different combinations, but as a rule only four are used.

Calculating with bits

Three bits will give you the following 8 combinations of ones and zeros:

0 000	4 100
1 001	5 101
2 010	6 110
3 011	7 111

The left-hand column contains decimal numbers with binary digits to the right. As you can see, these consist only of zeros and ones. Add 0 + 0 and the answer remains 0. Add 0 + 1, or 1 + 0 and the answer is 1. But what happens if you add 1 + 1? The answer cannot be 2, as the computer does not recognize this number. The answer to 1 + 1 is in fact 10.
In binary terms this means:

$0 + 0 = 0$
$0 + 1 = 1$
$1 + 0 = 1$
$1 + 1 = 10$

Multiplication can be even simpler:

$0 \times 0 = 0$
$0 \times 1 = 0$
$1 \times 0 = 0$
$1 \times 1 = 1$

AND, OR and NOT

The computer allows the use of three very important expressions: AND, OR and NOT. The NOT command always changes a zero into a one, and a one into a zero.

The OR command links two bits in such a way that a third bit is produced. If you enter two zeros, they will emerge as one zero; enter either one or two ones and a one will emerge.

The AND command produces a one if both entries are ones. Otherwise you will get a zero.

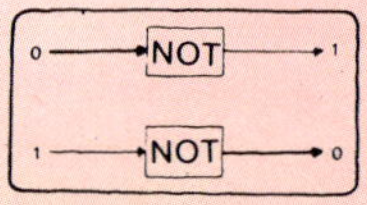

NOT-Command

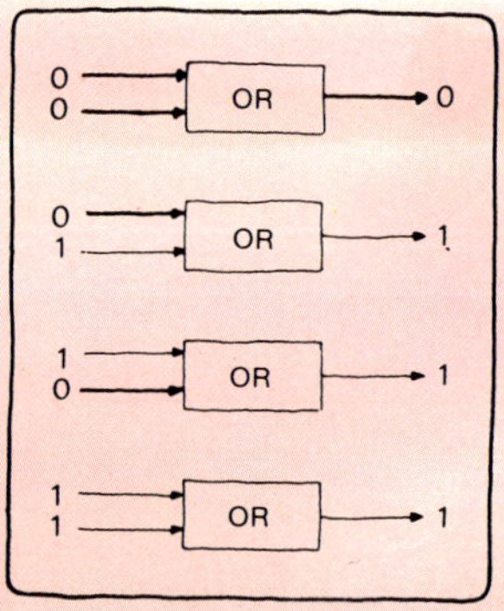

OR-Command

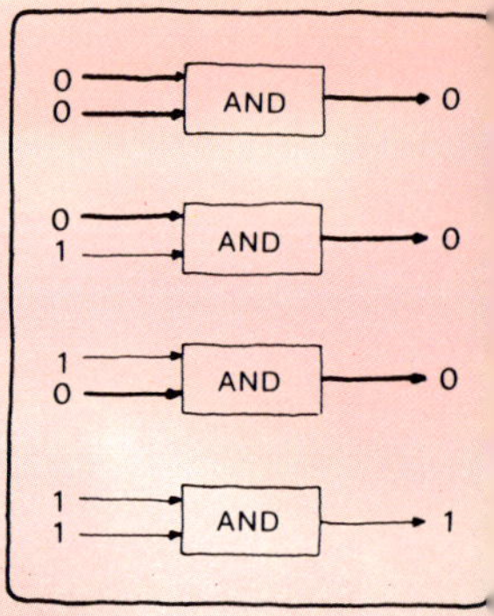

AND-Command

Letters, digits and bytes

Small computers work with data in groups of 8 bits known as 'bytes'. If you can write down all the possible combinations provided by 00000000 and 11111111 you will find the answer is exactly 256.

So each byte has the capacity to deal with 256 different characters. This is plenty to cover the usual keyboard collection of upper and lower case letters, decimal number and special symbols. In the computer, all these characters are translated into the language of off-on circuits, or ones and zeros. Type any letter on your keyboard and the computer will know which combination of on and off positions to select to produce the same letter on your screen.

Bits and bytes

OFF (0) or ON (1)

There are one hundred pence in a pound — and there are 8 bits in 1 byte. A page of typing paper holds 40 rows of 50 characters, representing 2000 bytes or 16 Kilobits.

A 500 page book has 500 × 2000 = 1 million bytes = 1 Megabyte = 1 Mbyte.

A small library with 1000 books has 1000 × 1,000,000 = 1,000 000,000 bytes = 1 thousand million or 1 Gigabyte = 1 Gbyte of information.

Electronic addition

When you join two bits with the AND command, you have in fact multiplied them. Addition requires a little more effort, and more circuits. The results might look as follows:

0 + 0 = 00
0 + 1 = 01
1 + 0 = 01
1 + 1 = 10

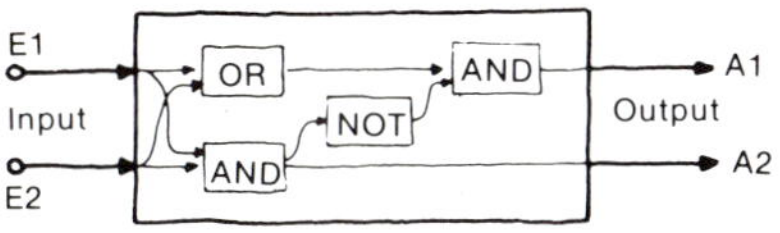

Our picture shows how bits are added together. If you wish to count in bytes or even greater number of bits, circuits will be correspondingly larger, as you need a memory space for each item. Calculations involving large numbers require a great many AND, OR and NOT circuits.

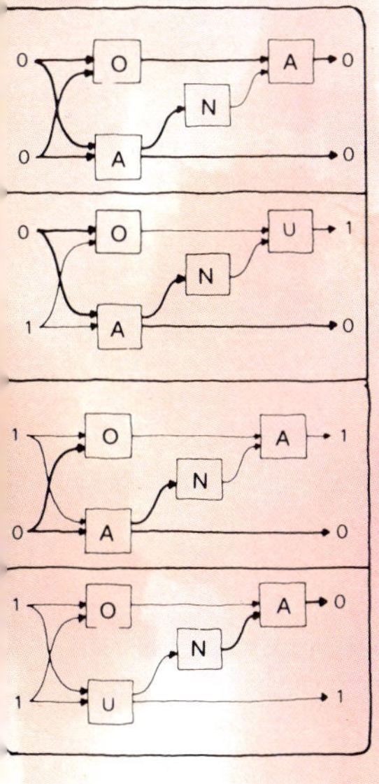

In-car warning lights

A dashboard indicator light can transmit two messages. For example:

0 Handbrake off (no light)
1 Handbrake on (light on).
Two such lights can transmit four messages:
00 All OK (both lights out)
01 Oil warning light (one light on, one off)
10 Battery charge warning (other light on, one off)
11 All incorrect (both lights on).

Traffic lights

These consist of three individual lights which can be switched on and off. They therefore require 3 bits, and could in fact transmit 8 messages. Five of these are necessary, but the others are not used.

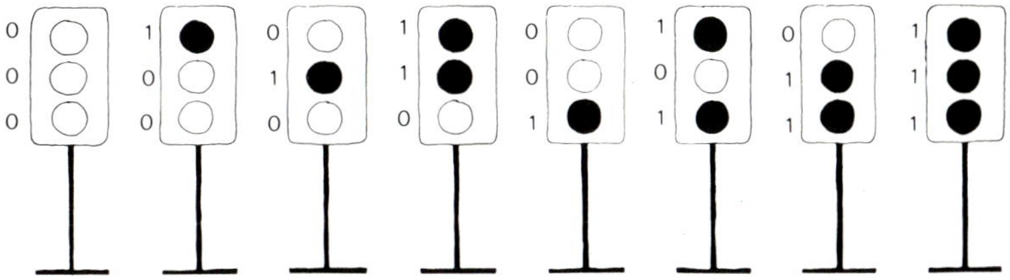

A glimpse inside

What can you see?

You can open up your micro and have a look inside. The manual will probably have a diagram or two showing how things work. Sometimes you have to open your computer — if you wish to expand it, for example. Inside you will see a flat base about the size of an envelope. This is the printed circuit board on which the computer is constructed. Micros vary from make to make, but there are similarities. For example, every micro has a Central Processing Unit (CPU) and some have more than one. The clock pulse inside the CPU is the basic unit of time, controlling the various cycles. The RAM and ROM are almost always made up of several components attached to the circuit board.

The input/output circuitry ensures that information is fed into and retrieved from the micro. There may also be ports for extension packs, for computer games or graphics for example. Additional items such as the power supply and disk drives are normally found outside the computer.

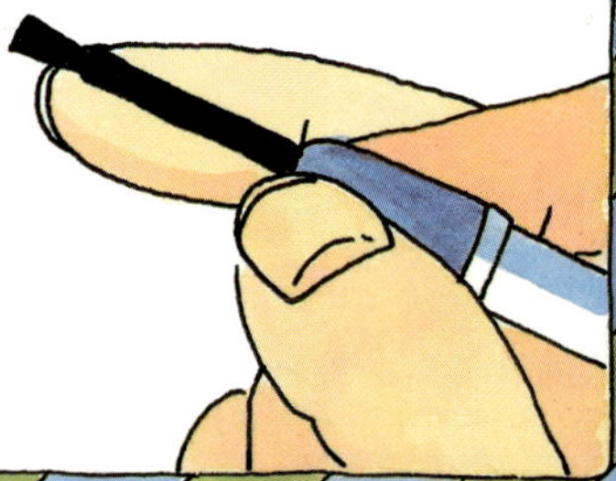

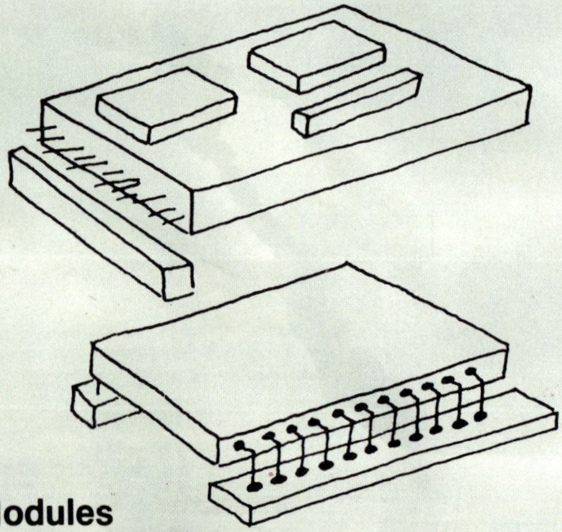

The circuit board

The circuit board carries electronic components. First the board is covered with a copper film onto which the connections between the various components are printed in different colours. The board is then dipped in acid which etches away the copper between the connections. This process is cheaper and more reliable than soldering individual wires.

Modules

Finished components are often referred to as 'modules'. For example, a RAM chip is a module. It fits into special sockets.

Since nothing needs soldering, you can fit extra chips yourself. Obviously you need clear instructions, either on the component itself or in your manual. Additional microprocessors are typical expansion modules, as are connections for further RAM or ROM chips. You may need to fit an extra switch to the board before you connect your new module. Follow the instructions carefully!

Input/output circuitry

Most larger micros contain a number of storage locations which start off blank. You can neither extract anything from them nor input anything until an expansion module is added. Now the micro can receive and transmit signals. For example, it can control the points and signals for an electric train set. Fitting some modules for example could ensure that.

2 Fitting new modules

Some circuit boards are designed to accommodate extra modules. In this case you will see a number of 'plugs', consisting of small, oblong plastic strips with holes to take the connectors. They are nearly always so arranged that there is only one correct way to fit the new modules. Don't use force! If it doesn't fit easily, it's not right!

3 The microprocessor

The microprocessor is the very heart and soul of the computer. In some ways it is like the engine in a car: it drives the whole computer. If you could see all the various connections you would realize that it is linked to the RAM as well as the ROM and the program commands. The processor understands these commands and ensures that they are carried out. Moreover, it can take in program data and process them.

When you are using the processor for arithmetical functions the data comes from the RAM. Sometimes extra help is needed from the ROM — for example, when Pi is involved. Because the microprocessor is so important we have devoted the whole of the next page to it.

The RAM

'ou can both write into and read from he RAM. You can expand the RAM to ake longer programs and more lata. Some micros allow you o insert extra RAM chips 'ourself.

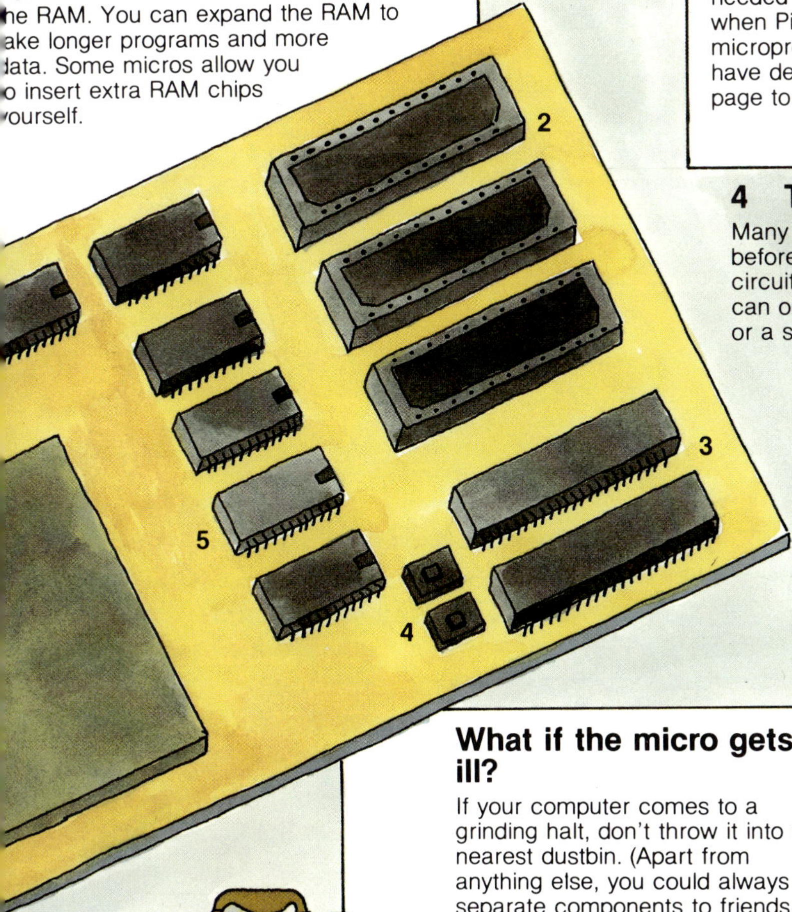

4 The switch

Many new modules need switching on before they will work. In this case your circuit board will carry tiny switches which can only be operated with a ballpoint pen or a similar shaped implement.

5 The ROM

The ROM is the memory from which we can read only — rather like a book. The computer manufacturer will already have filled the ROM with useful information. If you can expand the ROM in your computer, you can increase its BASIC instructions as well as adding other functions.

What if the micro gets ill?

If your computer comes to a grinding halt, don't throw it into the nearest dustbin. (Apart from anything else, you could always sell separate components to friends with the same machine!) Nor are pliers, and soldering irons necessary for repairing micros. Instead, your computer can display a test program telling you what is wrong. It could be that a RAM chip or other module has failed.

In this case, your manual will tell you what to do for the best. You may need to change a module or chip. With clear instructions this is something you can do yourself. And there will be no soldering! If the computer still refuses to function, take it back to the shop you bought it from. That way your machine will be attended to by experts.

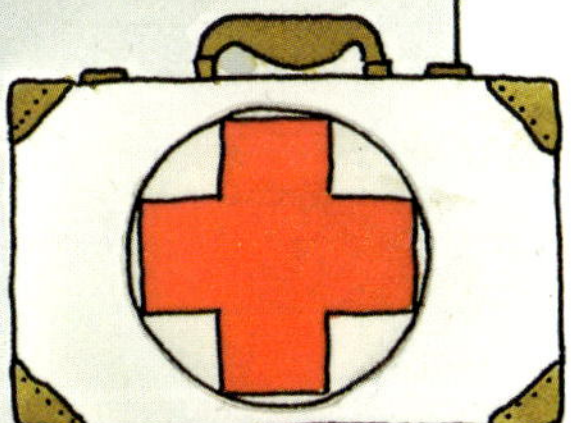

The microprocessor at work

The computer's microprocessor

The microprocessor 'drives' the computer rather as an engine drives a car. It is activated by orders which come either from the ROM or the RAM — depending on the nature of the task.

The processor fetches data from the RAM, processes it and returns it to RAM. The processor can also give commands of its own: for example it can arrange for data to be transmitted onto the screen or output via a printer. Or it can ensure data is transferred to disks for storage. The processor is responsible for all these events. So it is not only the driving force, it is the heart and soul of the computer. Earlier computers had processors built of transistors and integrated circuits. Since the advent of microelectronics processors have grown very small. For this reason they are now referred to as 'microprocessors'.

Hundreds of thousands of transistors can be fitted onto a chip no bigger than a finger nail.

What is a chip?

A chip is a tiny piece of silicon, smaller than a quarter of a centimetre square. Recent improvements in manufacturing and design mean that in many cases each tiny chip is in fact a computer on its own. A large number of electronic components and interconnections are integrated onto one chip of semiconductor material. Most chips are sealed in a plastic casing, oblong in shape, with a number of terminals or 'legs' sticking out from the two longer sides. Inside the casing each leg is connected with a communications wire, which you can in some cases see with the naked eye. Some chips are designed to store information, such as RAM and ROM chips, for example, and these are capable of holding 64K or more. Amazing as it may seem, there is room for hundreds of thousands of transistors on a single chip.

How fast is a microprocessor?

The speed at which a processor obeys commands depends upon the reaction speed of its circuits. Your handbook will tell you how many 'Instructions per Second' (IPSs) your microprocessor can handle. These are measured either in K thousand IPS (KIPS) or even in Mega IPS (MIPS). In other words, even a simple computer can handle thousands or millions of instructions per second.

Another factor is the number of bits the processor can handle at one time. An 8-bit processor can handle two parallel bytes. As you might imagine, a 16-bit processor is faster. You could test your computer's reaction speed by running the same program (in BASIC) on two different makes of machine. This would at least give you a rough comparison.

Memory storage

In order to function, the processor needs help from RAM and ROM chips. It feeds a particular address to the memory, and tells it whether to write into or read from.
The item to be processed is then held in a particular register of the processor.

Processing

The central processor chip gives the computer directions for all the basic steps it has to go through. This chip tells the machine to store, add to, compare and edit, and it also controls the order in which data and instructions are fetched from the memory.

The register

Registers are memories designed to hold a limited quantity of data — typically up to 64 bits. When an instruction has been selected from the memory, it is sent to the processor and temporarily stored in an 'instruction register'. From here, the instruction goes to a 'decoder' where it is translated into signals which carry out the required operation.

The instruction register

A byte selected from the memory is temporarily stored in an 'instruction register'. From here, the instruction goes to the decoder to be translated into signals which carry out the desired operation.

'he program counter

ıstructions cannot be fetched from the ıemory if their address is not known. or this reason all addresses are tored in a register in the processor nown as the program counter. Each pace in the program counter fits the ength of one address.

The interrupt function

Modern micros have a function enabling you to nterrupt the work of the processor. It makes a note of he exact point in the program vhere it has been requested o stop, and the user is then ree to attend to other matters. When you wish to eturn to the original task, it estarts at the point you left off.

The computer clock

In every computer, one process follows another. This is where the computer clock comes in. It acts rather like traffic lights at a road junction. But compared with the computer clock, traffic lights are extremely slow. A computer clock is capable of producing around 10,000 signals and impulses per second. It regulates the rate at which electrical impulses travel around the computer.
You can easily write a program which makes use of the clock generator's signals, and works out what time it is. Quartz watches work in this way too: they contain a very simple processor.

The data bus

ll the sections inside the microprocessor are connected to each other by a complex network of athways along which data, control and address buses' travel. When you type in a command, the nformation is picked up by one or other data bus and carried to the correct destination. If you want our computer to add a series of numbers together, he computer's Arithmetic and Logic Unit (ALU) is capable of taking two numbers at a time from your data and adding them 'serially'. Starting at one end and working its way along to the other, a bit at a ime.

The power supply

In order to function, the microprocessor needs a power supply. This comes from outside, and must first be transformed and distributed. Some computers come with their own plug-in power supply unit. Most micros require only a steady 5 volts and do not therefore use much electricity.

The decoder

Commands are held in the memory in letter form: 'GOTO' is a typical example. But the processor can only understand (1) and (0), representing electrical impulse (1), or no electrical impulse (0). This is where the decoder comes in. It translates commands into machine language.

Connectors

If you look very closely at a micro chip you will see a number of tiny wires. These are connected at one end to the various components of the microprocessor, and at the other to terminals. These in turn plug in to the sockets provided and allow electrical impulses to be transmitted.

You need software too

Programs, etc

Roughly speaking, 'hardware' is everything in the computer system that you can see and touch. 'Software' is the overall term for programs, processing procedures, data and stored information. We have already dealt with hardware in some detail and are now ready to move on to software. As you already know, programs have to be written in a language the computer understands — BASIC for example. But there are a great many other machine codes, each consisting of names, commands and data. These all come under the heading 'software'. In order to activate your micro you also need commands such as RUN or SAVE. These belong to the machine's retrieval system, and enable the processor to do its work.
You can buy additional software in the form of pre-programmed computer games, for example. Or you can buy blank disks or cassettes (sometimes referred to as raw software) and write your own programs.

BASIC

BASIC stands for Beginner's All-purpose Symbolic Instruction Code. It is a programming language built up of simple words and abbreviations. It is widely used and easy to learn.

FORTRAN

FORTRAN stands for FORmula TRANslator. It is a high-level computer programming language developed for scientific use. It uses many symbols and appears mathematical in form.

COBOL

COBOL stands for COmmon Business Oriented Language. Just as FORTRAN was designed for scientists, so COBOL is the businessman's computer language. Although it was designed for use on large computers, it is now spreading to micros.

APL

Believe it or not, APL is short for A Programming Language. It is another of the widely-used languages and is written in English or in mathematical symbols. It has its own command words, similar to those used in BASIC, which can be used to give the computer instructions to perform whatever type of operation you require. Compared to BASIC, APL appears extremely technical. Whereas BASIC, FORTRAN and COBOL operate via keywords, APL requires only individual symbols.

The compiler

The compiler is a complicated computer program that translates high level language into low level language — in other words, into something the machine can understand. The compiler which is also sometimes known as an 'assembler' has a number of uses, and can for example be used for checking spelling or grammatical errors. The words under scrutiny then comes up on your screen and it is up to you to make corrections or not.

The interpreter

The interpreter is another program which converts instructions in a high-level language such as BASIC into machine code. It then goes one step further and carries out the instruction one at a time. Many micros have an interpreter program built in. It then fetches the machine code it requires from the ROM.

Machine code

This is a set of instructions based on the construction of the computer's circuits. As we have seen, everything you type into the computer must be converted into ones and zeros. This may seem boring and cumbersome, but the computer can read each bit in about a millionth of a second, so it works extremely fast. The program you write is called the 'source program', the 'object program' is its binary, or machine code, form.

The operating system

This is software built into the computer making it possible for the user to communicate with the computer in a convenient way. For example, it might take the form of a set of instructions telling the computer how to perform functions such as communicating between screen, keyboard, disk and printer. The command RUN is often used, and if you key RUN 135 for example, the program you have called up will begin with line 135.
The operating system is usually built into the computer with a chip, but sometimes comes in disk form. Your handbook will tell you what is relevant to your computer.

Commands

A computer program consists of a series of commands which are carried out step by step until the STOP command is reached.
Other commands are different, in that they come directly from the user. For example, you might input a command for a correction to be made. The purpose of commands is to tell the computer how to work, and to make its workings more efficient. Your handbook will tell you which commands can be understood by your computer.

Ready-made programs

You can buy ready-made programs — some of them bearing striking or even outlandish titles — from software manufacturers. Programs of this kind are usually pre-packaged on disk or cassette and come with their own set of instructions. They vary from computer games to packages which will run a word processor.

Getting hold of programs

You don't have to write all your own programs

Without a program, a computer cannot work. But what's the best way of getting hold of programs? There are three ways:

1 Writing your own. This is easy if you know your micro well and what you want it to do. The more complicated the functions, the harder it is to program them yourself.

2 Buying programs. Some programs are too complicated for you to write yourself. Your local software dealer will stock a wide range of programs, suitable for many different micros. He will also be able to advise you on your particular needs.

3 Other peoples' programs. Programs can be obtained from friends and through computer clubs. You will also find new programs in the many computer magazines now available.

Manufacturers' programs

Most computer manufacturers produce programs as well as hardware. Your computer shop will probably be able to tell you what is available and where. Try to get hold of a book giving programs for you to type in to your micro. The book will show you how to check that you have entered the program correctly, so that it will run. Longer programs can be bought — often fairly cheaply — as cassettes or disks.

There are many shops that specialize in computer software and sell a range of cassettes, books and magazines.

Program data

Our program will process and produce data. It is useful to enter a typical data statement in order to check that the program is running correctly.

User programming

Programming can be fascinating. First you need to identify the individual items to be programmed, and then break them down into single steps. You then have to decide what data will be processed and what output will be required. It is a good idea to test a part of the program to see whether you have forgotten anything, or made any errors. When it is completed the program is printed out accompanied by notes — the technical term is 'documented' — so that other people can also use your program.

Data names

Data that is input to and output from the computer must be given a name. Two different items must have two different names. If not, you will disrupt the program and produce some peculiar results. For example, digits in BASIC must have different names from letters. Longer programs containing lots of data are best given related names — some people are very imaginative when it comes to inventing names.

Program compatibility

Two people using exactly the same computer will have no trouble swapping programs. But this is seldom the case. Different models of personal computers use different dialects of BASIC. Sometimes the variations can be fairly easily overcome. If a program you have borrowed contains instructions your micro does not recognize, you may still be able to load it if you use a little ingenuity.

Buying a program

It is a good idea to buy a program or a program package, but you need to make sure that it will run on your computer. It is not enough that it is written in a language your computer understands. There may be commands or instructions in the program that your micro cannot handle, so check first! Most programs are accompanied by a full description of their contents, and tell you how they are loaded into the micro, and how much RAM they occupy. There are usually instructions for checking the program as well.

Interactivity

The best programs involve the user in a dialogue or interaction with the computer. You communicate through the contents of screen or printer. The elements of this kind of dialogue need to be worked out carefully in advance, since changing them later will be difficult. Be brief and clear.

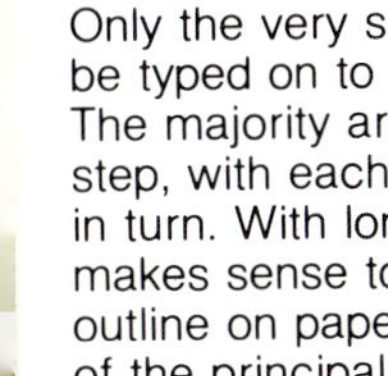

Testing

The program is finished when it will do what you want it to. You check this by testing the program with some test data, the results of which you already know. Where there are several branches to a program, each of them should be tested in the same way.

Testing is often a bit boring because you keep on coming across errors that you have to put right and then test again. In the final documentation of the program you should make a note of your test data. Even experienced programmers still find faults in their programs when they are retested later because some test element was overlooked.

Program outlines

Only the very simplest programs can be typed on to the screen in one go. The majority are built up step by step, with each part being checked in turn. With longer programs it makes sense to jot down a program outline on paper, and make a note of the principal steps. Do this in BASIC so as to avoid errors in logic.

Allow plenty of space in your outlines on paper — you've then got plenty of room to change your mind.

Documentation

For the end user a program is only as good as its documentation. Keep an exercise book or a file in which you write up the documentation for every program. How much memory is required? What programming language was used? Who wrote it and when? Test data are essential, as are details of running and loading times. Rough program outlines are best thrown away. It is not a good idea to give an undocumented program to anyone else.

Program libraries

Keeping track of lots of programs presents the same problem as finding records, cassettes or photographs. They are only useful if you can find them again. Again, a notebook or card index is invaluable. Your library should consist of ready-to-load programs. It is very time consuming to have to type in a whole program each time you want to use it: far better to store it on disk or cassette. Remember to keep your library system up to date, and keep a careful note of any changes or new acquisitions.

Buying a micro

Micro prices

Buying a micro needs as much thought as buying a car. Even when you are being given a micro as a present, you should be involved in making the choice. The first thing to decide on is the size of the machine. There are micros the size of pocket calculators costing under £100. Some include a mini-printer.

Larger micros can cost up to £5,000. These are very well made and are suitable for professional and business use.

In between lies a huge range of machines, and detailed comparisons are found in many computer magazines. Many micros can be expanded by the addition of extra RAM, a printer, or disk drives for example. The more expensive your micro, the surer you must be that it is what you want. Make sure too that your machine carries a good guarantee and that it offers efficient after-sales service. (More about that on the next page.)

Small home computers

The smallest computers are not unlike larger pocket calculators. They can be programmed in BASIC and have a 400-word memory. They are excellent machines, especially for young people embarking on their first microcomputer.
Many of these computers can be expanded with 16K RAM extensions. Printers using small rolls of paper can be attached, as can cassette recorders for storage of programs and other data. Depending on size, age and model, these will cost between £50 and £400. Their processors are not very powerful — just as the smallest car engines are not very powerful — but they do go!

Middle range micros

Middle range micros will have at least one disk drive and around 64K or RAM. They may have their own screen and a built-in cassette recorder. Further disk drives can be added so that you can build up a large library of programs on disk. Micros in this range often have the CPU, RAM and ROM, keyboard, screen and disk drive in one cabinet, and cost around £750. Printers and other peripherals can be added later.

Quality and guarantees

Quality is obviously related to price, but also to the speed and ease with which the machine can be repaired when something goes wrong. Components and replacement parts should be readily available, especially for the more expensive computers which are probably used more frequently.

When buying a micro you should enquire about parts and service and make sure you have a written guarantee. Modern computers are very reliable, but you must know where you stand.

Computer bench tests

Trying to compare two different micros is a pretty hopeless exercise. Bench tests have been devised to help in the process. The same BASIC program is run on all the micros on test. Running time, speed of memory search and other characteristics are noted. If the program won't run, investigations are made to find out whether the micro uses a different BASIC dialect, or there are 'bugs' in that particular program. But while bench tests will provide some basis for comparison, the final decision is usually a matter of personal choice.

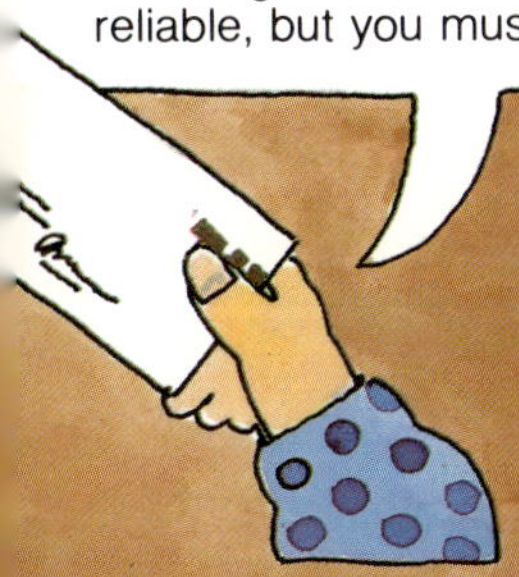

Technology and power

The large number of microcomputers available today make use of a huge range of technological processes. As a result, the quality of every component — from power supply to printer output — can vary from one machine to another. Make sure that all the leads and connections fit snugly, or your machine's performance may be adversely affected. With some machines replacement batteries can cost almost as much as the original micro which can get very expensive. The watchword is: look before you buy!

The big micros

A calculator which has a single chip processor is a microcomputer of sorts. When the processor can be programmed by the user in BASIC or a similar language the machine can be thought of as a personal computer. It is difficult to establish rigid divisions between personal and business microcomputers since many personal computers can now be linked into networks, or receive teletext and viewdata information systems via telephone or television.

The biggest micros have 16-bit processors (and soon probably 32-bit) and usually 1 Megabyte of memory. In these machines the processor, memory and disk drive are usually built into a single cabinet, but the keyboard and screen are kept separate so that they can be adjusted for ease of use.

You will find more helpful hints on buying a microcomputer on the next page.

More hints on buying a micro

Think before you buy

Buying anything but the cheapest mini micro is a serious matter. It's not just a question of cost and appearance, as it might be with a television or a typewriter. If you buy a more expensive microcomputer, you are likely to be stuck with it for a long time, and will have to live with its particular characteristics. On this page are a few more helpful tips.

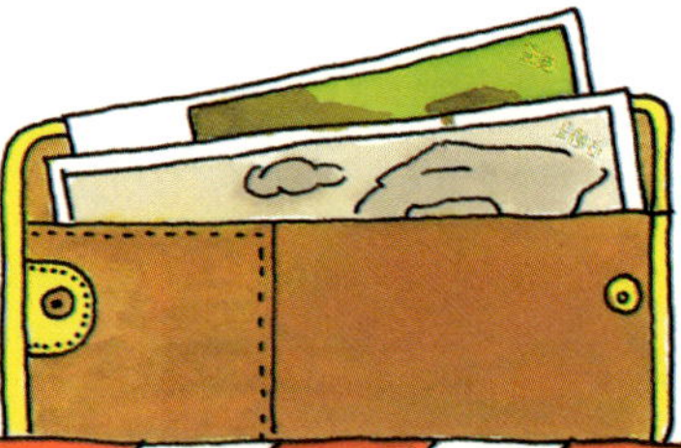

Software counts too

The computer is only as good as its programs. They prove the machine's value to the user. When buying a computer it is essential to check that the range of software you are likely to need exists for that model. Software costs money and you must make sure that your chosen machine is well provided for.

The computer handbook

A computer is only as good as its handbook. A good handbook should have a detailed index, clear instructions, lots of examples and a logical progression through the functions of the machine. As you become more experienced, you will need the handbook less and less, but even the greatest expert sometimes feels the need to check back! So look carefully at the handbooks when you are comparing machines.

Hands-on experience

It's a good idea to try to use any computer you're thinking of buying. Computers bought by mail order therefore need even more careful consideration. You will often find that a friend somewhere has the computer you're thinking of buying. See if he/she will let you try it out, and ask for any useful hints. That way you should be able to satisfy yourself on some of the important questions that need to be answered before you buy.
There are many shops where you can try out a range of micros before buying.

Printers

Printers present similar problems to screens. The number of dots the printer can produce in each row and column has an effect on print quality. Make sure the print quality is adequate for your purposes. How well does the printer reproduce what was on the screen? There can be disappointing distortions, especially with graphics. Many printers will only handle letters and numbers, and their graphics capability is therefore very limited. However, the printing of letters from the keyboard should present no problems.

All about screens

Before buying a monitor, check that it will do everything you want of it. Remember that looking at a screen for any length of time can be extremely tiring, so choose one that is easy on your eyes. If you intend using a lot of graphics, go for a screen with the maximum number of pixels. Then there is the question of colour. Can the screen handle three, eight, sixteen or even more colours? Testing screens is a matter of looking carefully. But even with the best monitors you can only achieve what the programming language allows.

'he more memory the better

ıe amount of memory on board the micro is ıportant — can the RAM be expanded and at hat cost? With cassettes you have to remember ıe disadvantages compared with disks: data and ·ograms have to be read and written one fter the other. With disks we are looking at apacities in Kilobytes, and access times in ıilliseconds — and more capacity and ıorter access times make for better disks. Larger ıicros have built-in hard disk storage. They are xpensive but give great capacity and rapid access me. Since you cannot change the contents of hard isks, you load data from them into the micro's ıemory at the beginning of your run, just as you ·ould from cassettes or floppy disks.

Applications by the dozen

Larger micros can receive, process and transmit signals. They can be programmed to read meters and open and close valves. They can control the operation of a model train set. The list goes on and on, but most of these applications are outside the scope of this book. If you are really interested in this aspect you should talk to your computer dealer.

Big and little brothers

The personal computer

The micro is the modern-day equivalent of the slide rule. It has all the characteristics of large computers and is in every sense a real computer. It does not differ in any significant way from its bigger brothers used in industry, research laboratories or universities except in power and speed of handling programs. It is a valuable member of the same family.

The business computer

Many businesses benefit considerably from the use of a computer. The computer can prepare invoices, record payments and keep the company's accounts in order. It can work out the monthly wage and salary payments and keep the company's balance sheets up to date. Many small firms use personal computers to carry out work of this kind.

The scientific computer

Computers have an important role to play in science and engineering where there are many complicated calculations to be made. Remember too that plans, diagrams and models can be displayed on computer screens. And computers can also be used in factories work out the most efficient way of producing goods. These computers are no different from others: they ar just programmed differently.

Using data banks

Where a number of people need access to large amounts of stored data at the same time, the computer manages the data bank. It controls access to the data, retrieves it and displays it on the screen. For example, a bank clerk can check whether a customer has enough money in his credit account to make a withdrawal. Access to this data is controlled by a secret number known only to the customer and the bank. With modern micros it is possible to gain access to large data banks if you have the right connections.

Computers working together

Modern computers often work together — for example, all the computers owned by a bank. They can transmit and receive data to and from each other through telephone links. Much financial information can be passed directly through such a network.

Micros can also gain access to large computers by dialling a telephone number and making the right connection. The larger computer will give instructions and the micro will engage in a dialogue with its bigger brother. Several micros can also be joined together in a local area network.

index

glossary

BASIC — Beginners' All-purpose Symbolic Instruction Code: a special language used for programming computers.

BEEP — A computer programming command in BASIC which is used to produce sound from a microcomputer.

BIT — An abbreviation for Binary digit, 0 or 1.

BYTE — A group of 8 bits which form a computer word.

CHIP — A common word for assemblies of electronic components on tiny squares of silicon. They may be microprocessors or storage or memory chips.

COMPILER — A program which translates input in BASIC or similar languages into machine code, i.e. the strings of 0s and 1s which are all the computer can process.

CURSOR — A device which appears on the screen to indicate where material input through the keyboard will be positioned.

DELETE — A command which erases unwanted material.

DIRECTORY — A listing of all the contents of a storage system.

ENTER — A command which puts what has been typed into the computer's memory.

FORTRAN — An abbreviation of FORmula TRANslator — a programming language.

GET — A command which retrieves information from the computer memory.

GOTO — A command which tells the computer to jump to a particular line of a program and carry out the function listed there.

INTERPRETER — A program which converts languages such as BASIC into machine code step by step.

LIST — A command which causes all the lines of instructions that make up a program to be displayed.

LOAD — An instruction which causes material stored on tape or disk to be transferred to the computer's memory.

MEMORY — The part of a computer where data can be stored and retrieved.

PRINT — A command which causes items in a program to be printed out on the screen or on a printer.

RANDOM ACCESS — Computer memory which can have data added to it and retrieved from it.

READ ONLY — Computer memory from which data can only be retrieved and not added to.

RENUMBER — A command which shuffles the line numbers of a program.

RUN — An instruction which starts the operation of a program.

SAVE — A command which causes material to be stored in the computer memory or on tape or disk.

SHIFT — The use of the shift and other keys on the keyboard gives many of them different functions.